POWER OF THOUGHT

**How to Control What
Happens to You**

Eugene Maurey

Published by Midwest Books
4555 W. 60th Street
Chicago, Illinois 60629 USA

ABOUT THE AUTHOR

Eugene Maurey is founder and president of the Maurey Instrument Corporation in Chicago. His company, founded in the basement of his apartment building in 1953, has become one of the leading manufactures of electro-mechanical components for the aerospace and automation industries. He was a captain of artillery in WW II, serving in the European Theater of Operations, 1944-1945. He is an author and stimulating lecturer on metaphysics, exorcism and unorthodox healing.

Printed in the United States of America
First printing: 1990
Second printing: 1994

ISBN: 0-9626906-2-7

Published by Midwest Books
4555 W. 60th Street
Chicago, Illinois 60629

This book may be purchased from the publisher.
Please include $1.00 for postage and handling.

This book is affectionately

dedicated to Peace Pilgrim,

my teacher and friend.

ACKNOWLEDGEMENT

I have been fortunate to have friends familiar with the subject of this book and their thought provoking questions and suggestions has forced me to clarify for you, the reader, the thoughts expressed in this book. I am deeply grateful to Dr. Leonid Kovalesky of Palos Verdes Estate, to my daughter-in-law, Carol Maurey of Milville, Canada, to Editor Rose LeVan of East Chicago, to Professor Maria Widmanska of Barcelona, Spain, and to Mary McCall of Chicago, Illinois

Cover by: Anthony W. Filipowski
Crown Point, Indiana

WHY THIS BOOK WAS WRITTEN

Like many of you, I stumbled through life taking the good and the bad as it came. I had little control over what happened to me; it was a mixture of coincidence and luck, good or bad. There was sickness and health, a good marriage and a bad one, prosperity and desperate need. Most of us have gone through similar experiences and we wonder why we have no better control over our destiny.

At the age of 55 I finally started to get a handle on how to control what happens to me; I blundered into the subject called metaphysics. Nobody gave me that name for it then. People I met simply demonstrated to me how their minds worked. I met persons who apparently could heal using but their minds. I met others who most certainly were reading my thoughts. There were even those who apparently were influencing the weather!

I discovered that there are many books written on metaphysics, the psychic, spiritual healing and religion. I began to read and seek teachers who could answer the questions what my life was all about.

Being an engineer, the solutions to my problems had to be practical and repeatable. When I expected something to happen, I couldn't say, "Maybe it will happen." It had to happen.

My road to learning has had few shortcuts and along the way I made many mistakes. Now, some 18 years later, with most of the garbage cleared from my mind, I can begin to speak of practical measures that a person can take to have a better and happier life and to avoid the down-slides of the past. This is what this book is all about.

Eugene Maurey, 1990

CONTENTS

POWER OF THOUGHT

CHAPTER 1

UNRAVELING A MIRACLE

THE FLYING CARPET

Have you ever found yourself in a dangerous situation and gotten out of it without knowing what had happened? Unknowingly you were using the most powerful force in the Universe. Let me relate an experience I had some years ago when the enormity of this power was first made unmistakably clear to me.

On returning home one evening, after a particularly heavy snow storm and sudden freeze, I found myself on what appeared to be a clear, perfectly safe, six-lane expressway. I increased my speed up to 55 miles per hour; then the unexpected happened. The car began to skid sideways on a sheer, icy road! I lightly touched the brakes; I turned the wheel. There was no response. My first thought was, "Here I go smashing up this beautiful white car!" Immediately dismissing the thought, I looked up and mentally said, "Take over!"

Knowing all was well, I relaxed and let my hands rest lightly on the steering wheel. In what appeared to be a split second, the car traveled another 50 yards and drove itself into a soft snow bank, missing steel road guards and a lamp post by a wide margin. Perplexed, I looked around me; the car had suddenly stopped yet my body had felt no forward motion. My hands still rested without pressure on the steering wheel! It was simply that at one moment the car was spinning on the road completely out of control and in the next instant it had transported itself to the snow bank. Thankfully, I took a deep breath of relief.

When I told others of my mystifying experience, several persons were pleased to find someone who could relate to an unusual experience they had. One such person, Dolores Henleben, had long been hesitant to tell of her experience. She related the following extraordinary story:

"At an intersection when driving my car I made a wrong turn. A speeding car driven by a woman headed directly at me; I could see an expression of terror in her eyes. A disastrous collision seemed inevitable. I thought, `Oh, my poor children will be without a mother'. Instantly, I found myself seated in my car which was undamaged and parked in a supermart parking lot about 100 yards from the intersection! I could not account for what had happened. I felt no one would believe me if I told such a fantastic story so spoke to no one. You are the first to hear about this."

During a recent discussion of this subject, a friend, Carol McKinney, related to me her unexplainable experience. "Last night I was driving," she said, "on this dark and quite icy road. Without warning as I entered a bridge two cars collided at the center of the bridge, completely blocking the road in front of me. My brakes did not respond. I headed directly toward the two cars at full speed. And then a miracle happened. I was no longer on the bridge, the bridge was behind me and I found myself driving down the road!"

One more anecdote. During a lecture when I spoke of my miraculous escape, a man suddenly exclaimed, "That explains what happened to me." He was given the floor. "I was driving this semi with trailer on a particularly dark night on a narrow two-lane road. Suddenly my headlights picked up a car stalled across both lanes. There were people in it. I couldn't stop and couldn't avoid hitting it. I closed my eyes and tensed for the impact. Nothing happened. I opened my eyes. The car was not in front of my truck. I glanced in my rear view mirror. The car was *behind* me still across the road in the same position where I had first seen it!"

Miracles? Possibly. Yet we know that a miracle is only something for which we have no rational explanation and when we solve the puzzle, it is no longer a miracle.

These examples may possibly be understood when we understand the laws governing such events. These laws are the invisible nonmaterial laws grouped under the general subject of Metaphysics.

A LAW: WHAT IS IT?

A law by definition states: *A cause will always produce a predictable effect.* It is impartial in its action. When rightly used, it is your servant. It always works.

Perhaps a law can best be explained through the following illustration: If a pencil is held up and then released, it predictably falls to the floor. This always happens, as it follows a physical law, in this case the Law of Falling Bodies, commonly called the Law of Gravity.

Also, should you step from a flying airplane, you fall. The law doesn't care whether you a have a parachute on or not. It doesn't matter whether you are good or bad, white or black, male or female. The law *always* works. It is nondiscriminating and impartial. Most laws with which we are acquainted are physical laws. Other laws of importance to our lives are the nonphysical laws - the Laws of Metaphysics.

WHAT IS METAPHYSICS?

Webster defines metaphysics as..."a systematic study

of the fundamental nature of reality going beyond and above what we know as physical reality." *In this book metaphysics is interpreted as those laws that are always acting to produce the manifestations of our thinking, either in a positive or negative way.*

THE 3 PARTS OF THE MIND

What is metaphysics? Just how does it work? To simplify the explanation, we must understand the relationship of the three parts of the mind, the Conscious Mind, the Subconscious Mind and the Superconscious Mind.

THE CONSCIOUS MIND

The Conscious Mind is that portion of the mind (as distinct from the brain) which weighs the inputs and facts available to make decisions.

The input to the conscious mind is from the five physical senses: sight, hearing, touch, smell and taste. The conscious mind operates in the waking state. It deals with the physical world. It is that part of the mind which does the thinking, reasoning, doubting, guessing, evaluation and judging. *Most important - the conscious mind is the decision maker.*

The conscious mind does not create. It is like the

skilled machinist who builds a machine from the carefully drawn mechanical design created by the design engineer.

THE SUBCONSCIOUS MIND

The Subconscious Mind is also known as the subjective or the unconscious. This is the area of the mind where all emotions and feelings reside.

Within the subconscious mind are the emotions of love, peace, loyalty, joy, patriotism, appreciation of the arts, anger, hatred, greed - to name a few. Also, this is where all memory resides. The subconscious remembers everything. Under hypnosis a subject can recall complete conversations he had made years earlier. *The subconscious comes into play when a person is in deep thought or is concentrating. Unlike the conscious mind, it cannot make decisions.*

The conscious mind governs the subconscious. Whatever the input into the subconscious, whether right or wrong, the subconscious will act upon it and create those conditions that the conscious mind ordered. To direct the subconscious effectively, one must take great care to clarify what is wanted.

How does the subconscious makes things happen for you? Not only is it the seat of all feelings and the repository of memory, it also serves as the direct link to the Superconscious Mind, where all power and infinite intelligence is -

the Creative Power, the Source where the work is done.

THE SUPERCONSCIOUS MIND

The Superconscious Mind is that part of the mind which possesses infinite intelligence and all creative power, available everywhere all the time.

Albert Einstein (1879-1955), physicist, described the Superconscious Mind "as the ultimate formula of all that exists." Others define it as the Cosmic Intelligence that governs all things. It is the Prime Source of all that comes into being. What is important to understand is that under the right circumstance this intelligence and power are available to you and to all human beings.

Nothing is terribly new about this concept of the Superconscious Mind. Two thousand years ago It was described as Omnificent - unlimited in creative power, as Omnipotent - unlimited authority or influence, and as Omnipresent - present in all places at all times.

THE RELATIONSHIP BETWEEN THE 3 PARTS OF THE MIND

The following diagram is an explanation of how we are able to tap into this power and intelligence and produce the desired events in our lives.

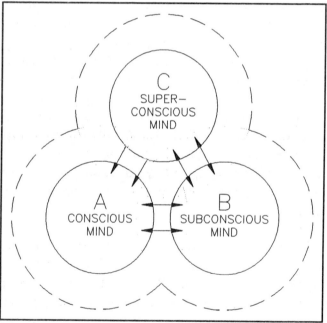

Figure 1

Communication normally flows from A to B to C and the reverse from C to B to A.

Under extraordinary circumstances, communication can flow directly from A to C or from C to A.

Although it may appear that the three parts of the Mind are separate, in reality there is no separation, but complete unity.

This is precisely how the system works: When the conscious self needs information, guidance or help of any kind, the subconscious is directed to produce the results. When that level of mind is convinced that you mean business, the message is shipped up to the Superconscious which in turn delivers the goods. The path is fixed.

Only occasionally can you put in your order directly to the Superconscious Mind. Apparently for myself and the others the conditions were right for our vehicles to be instantly transported out of harm's way. There was an instantaneous response by the Superconscious Mind. (Refer to Figure 1)

Note: The instantaneous movement of persons and objects over distances may be more widely experienced than is generally known. There are frequent reports of apports where an object either suddenly disappears or appears. How this occurs and where it goes or from where it comes is unknown.

When we understand, in a practical sense, how we can apply the laws of metaphysics, we can begin to direct our minds for positive results. In the next chapter we will examine those laws which are of special help to us.

CHAPTER 2

HOW THE LAW WORKS

LAW OF THOUGHT

The first important law explains why we have complete control of our life and every event in it. It is called the *Law of Thought*. The law simply states: ***Whatever you think and believe, that is what you will experience.*** As you think you create. All that happens around you is the effect of your thinking. The quality of your life is entirely due to your thinking. Your thoughts create the things and events in your life.

If, then, your thoughts govern your experience, you may question the extent to which you were led to read this book. Is it possible there is something written here which is important to you at this moment? Could it also be possible that the author was led to write these ideas for you in particular as a result of your thoughts and desires? It could well be so.

We shall limit our discussion to those laws of metaphysics to which you can readily relate in your everyday experiences.

PARKING NO PROBLEM!

Let me give a brief example of how I use the power of thought almost everyday. I frequently have occasion to park in large shopping malls where it is difficult to find a parking place. Knowing this, I usually will stop 5 or 10 minutes before arrival at my destination and mentally see my car parked in the best spot available. Almost without exception a place will be there waiting for me, the perfect parking place.

WATCH THOSE NEGATIVE THOUGHTS!

On another more recent occasion I used the Power against myself. I observed that I was tripping over things. I said to a friend, "I'm tripping over things, I have to be more careful. *I'll hurt myself.*" Two days later I indeed tripped over an obstacle and incapacitated myself for two weeks!

There are expressions that we all have used and unknowingly have harmed ourselves. A shortcut to aches and pain is to complain, "He gives me a pain in the neck!" Another common one: "Oh, my aching back!" Or worse: "She gives me a headache!" Your subconscious believes literally what you say and does exactly as it is told.

Great care must be practiced in what you think and say. If you desire good things, positive thoughts in that direction will create them for you. If you think something can happen, it will happen. The key to neutralizing a negative thought is to acknowledge its possibility but to add the thought, "But it won't happen to me!" Some people use the expression, "Cancel, Cancel!" to clear their minds of a negative thought. Wouldn't it be great to have only good things happen to you!

As a young man, I was unaware of how the mind worked. As illustrated by the following story, I made some fearsome mistakes.

A HOT SPOT

During World War II, I was a forward artillery observer, a profession that was far from dull. On one occasion I drove out to a location which the enemy would later most likely occupy. Nearby I ordered a round of artillery to be fired to register our guns. (After a known location was accurately fired upon, all adjacent targets could be accurately pinpointed.) On this occasion the enemy made a fast getaway and my order was cancelled. At the time I asked myself the question: "If I had been standing on the target that I had selected would the first round of artillery have hit me?" I then dismissed the thought and hurried off to my next assignment.

The seed had been planted in my subconsious mind: It thought, "So he really wants to sit on a target and get shot at; I'll fix it for him."

Several weeks later I was assigned the unlikely task of acting as a safety officer for our front line troops. Our artillery battalion wished to practice shooting in a large area *behind* our infantry. The base point (the point to register our guns) was given to me as a point on a map. I went forward to our front line troops, turned around and looked for the preselected target.

The wooded area in which I found myself apparently obscured the target. To see better, I climbed up on an 8 foot high brick wall, stood up and scanned the area with my binoculars. I still could not locate the target. After a futile search, I thought, "What the hell, I'll fire a round and see where it lands." I gave the command. Less than a minute later the shell came screaming straight at me, passed over my head and exploded 20 yards behind me! With a great deal of profanity, I shouted the command to cease firing! It was a perfect hit; I was standing on the target!

Moral: Don't ask yourself a foolish question; the answer may kill you.

POWER OF A NEGATIVE THOUGHT

Often an unknown element can be a stumbling block to your success. Negative persons may be around you who with their negative thinking are either quietly or loudly negating everything that you are trying to do. A negative thought follows the same law as a positive one. *Whatever a negative person thinks and believes will surely manifest in his/her world.* Such thoughts can be powerful indeed. Therefore, one must ever be vigilant to guard against the negative thinking of others.

Negative people in your personal life or in your work place do much to destroy the success of what you wish to accomplish. Such people in business are a burden to the operation, retarding both the progress and prosperity of the business. Speaking from experience, my advice is to run when you see them coming!

Let me give you an actual case. In my business the people are positive minded. Their vocabularies are devoid of such words as "if", "maybe", "perhaps" or "I'll try." As a result of their positive mental attitude, the business is doing well.

There was a short period when our business began to falter, sales and profits began to drop off. We had hired a highly technical man who apparently knew little of the value of positive thinking. His negative thoughts had a devastating effect on almost everyone in the company and even extended to our customers. He was asked to leave. Shortly afterwards sales resumed their earlier upward spiral.

WHY TAKE LESS THAN THE BEST

On a more positive note, a young Polish lady came to this country with only $50 in her purse and not knowing a word of English. She soon found work cleaning offices which required transportation. She bought a junker for $50. She began to fantasize what it would be like to own a Mercedes. Before long she sold the the junker for $75 and bought another car for $150. Selling that car for $250 she bought a slightly better car. It took her three years but her seventh car was a late model Mercedes.

As illustrated above, everything is associated with how you think, how your mind works. Understanding the laws of metaphysics becomes the key to controlling what happens to you.

There is a truism: If someone can do something, you can do it - and do it better. In the next chapter we will meet such people who understand and use these laws to attain a better life for themselves.

CHAPTER 3

PRACTICING THE MYSTERY

VISUALIZATION

One of the most powerful tools you can use to speed up the process of achieving a desire is to visualize what you want as already being yours. The key to effective visualization is putting a great deal of feeling into it. Successful visualization is accomplished as follows:

(1) Believe that you have what you desire now, not in any future time. (If you place in the future what you want that is where it will remain, in the future. Time does not exist.)

(2) Put into your belief strong feelings of love, joy, harmony, prosperity, great satisfaction or other positive emotion associated with the event.

(3) Concentrate on having what you desire. If you have done the first two steps correctly your concentration was perfect.

(4) Don't *ask* that your desire be fulfilled, *expect* it.

Warning! Be careful *not* to think of a specific solution that you think would be best. You may get it and find that it isn't what you wanted. Think of the solution, whatever it is, as giving you a great deal of satisfaction and joy, then all the conditions will be met to bring about the positive result desired. Let the Superconscious Mind work out the details.

HOW NOT TO BUY A CAR

Let us first examine what not to do as illustrated by the following example. A man desired a particular yellow Cadillac convertible. Knowing something about the power of his thoughts, he visualized himself buying it, being seated in it and driving it around town. Soon afterward to his delight he saw the identical Cadillac in a used car lot and bought it. It was not long before he discovered that the carburetor had to be rebuilt, a new muffler and tail pipe were needed and the starter and alternator had to be replaced.

Finally, after the Cadillac mechanic had examined the knocking engine he turned to the owner and announced, "This car is a lemon, a yellow one!"

The man's error was to visualize the *details* of the car and not the *qualities* he desired in a car. Qualities are in the *feelings* department.

He should have visualized the Cadillac in this way: He sees himself driving this *beautiful* Cadillac, he *likes* the bright yellow color, he is *satisfied* with the price he paid for it, he is *pleased* with the *smoothness* of the drive and he is *aware* that it is in *perfect* mechanical condition. He *feels safe* with the *excellent* tires it has and he *knows* it gives *good* gas mileage. He sees his friends *admiring* the exterior and interior of the car. He *feels very comfortable and quite content* with his good car. Note everything is in the present, all pertains to feelings or to the subconscious subjective part of the mind. The only actual specification is the make and color of the car.

Simply stated, when you have a desire, visualize the *feelings* that you have when that desire is satisfied. Keep your visualization in the present time. As an added bonus you will discover many plus features when your desire materializes, few of which could have been anticipated.

USING THE LAW

Again refer to figure 1. We note the interesting relationship between the three parts of our mind but what is not immediately apparent is that the Superconscious Mind is the same Mind that we all have. This means that we are all of that Mind; it can't be doled out a little here and little there. The conclusion must be that if this is so - that we are sharing together this same Mind - then you know all about me and I know all about you. Being a sound business man this makes sense to me and I use the notion of a Universal Mind in my business and in many other areas of my life. Let me illustrate this.

HOW TO BE A SUPER SALESMAN

I have a secret to share with you.

In my electro-mechanical business one of my responsibilities is sales. Betty, my secretary, will occasionally remind me, "Mr. Maurey, we could use more sales!"

"OK," I reply, "I'll take care of it immediately!" Three minutes later I report back to Betty, "It's done, sales are on the way."

This is what I do. Just as I am part of the great Universal Mind, I assume that all our present and future customers are also part of it. I contact them. Seating myself in a comfortable chair, I relax and close my eyes. I then visualize new orders spilling over onto my desk with the resulting pleasurable feeling of prosperity and interesting activity. I know that each order is for the mutual benefit of both ourselves and the customer. I see delighted smiles of satisfaction on the faces of Betty and our superintendent. As an added measure I see the pleased expression on the face of our comptroller when he examines our books. Finally, I dismiss everything from my mind. Within hours, orders are phoned in to us; in days we are inundated with business.

PLACE YOUR ORDER!

All too often I meet salespersons or people in their own business who have little success. After conversing with them, I conclude that such people work hard and have all the attributes required for success. Should you fit into this category the first question I would ask you is, "Would you like more business?" Most likely your reply would be, "Yes!"

Here is what you can do. Each morning upon arising, sit quietly in a place where you will not be disturbed. Visualize yourself that evening feeling good about all the wonderful things that happened to you that day. See your friends and family being very pleased with your accomplishments. You may wish to ham it up and see yourself jumping up and down with great joy. *Do not specify what is to happen!* After you have done this, forget it and let it happen to you. Forgetting may at first be difficult to do but it is very important in this process.

Wonderful events will begin to happen to you. Usually there will be no sudden change. It will come gradually. Whatever it is that gives you a *feeling* of great pleasure starts to manifest in your life. If it is sales you desire, it will eventually pour down on you from every direction. If it is a special friendship, the person will appear. If it is information, within days it will be laid out before you.

At first, you may experience little success in this

meditation. When you persist, within a week there will be evidence that something is happening. Within a month you will be flying!

As you increase your belief that this process is working for you, you will experience increasing success. At first you will be a novice in this procedure, but at each evidence of success your confidence will grow and you can expect even greater successes. Be patient. You will succeed. We crawl before we walk.

THE IMPORTANCE OF FORGETTING

When we first start thinking about applying the laws of the mind to our daily tasks and problems, many of us have doubts. You follow the instructions to the letter; you relax, you have a good idea what you wish to accomplish, you put feeling into it and expect it to happen. You have done everything correctly. Later you say to yourself, "Perhaps I missed something. Did I do anything wrong? Maybe it won't hurt to review my thoughts and perhaps do the work better."

Do your programming once and then completely dismiss it from your mind. Forgetting is the most difficult thing you must learn to do.

If you planted a seed, would you keep digging it up to see if it is growing?

WITH A LITTLE CARE, A ROSE WILL GROW ANY-WHERE

Here is an narrative that has a happy ending. Some years ago I asked for an IBM salesperson to call on us to demonstrate the latest IBM typewriter.

A charming young black lady named Ann called. In the course of our conversation, I asked, "How are you doing on sales?" She dropped her head and looked at her folded hands. "Not so good." she replied.

"Would you like to do better? I asked.

She brightened, "I certainly would!"

I then explained the process above and within an hour she left. We did not order the typewriter.

About 18 months later we requested Ann to call on us. We were ready to order the typewriter.

As soon as Ann saw me she exclaimed, "Am I glad to see you!" She then went on to explain that when she had first called on us in October, she had only been working as a salesperson for two months and her sales were far below her quota. In November her sales jumped to 300 percent of her quota.

I asked, "What happened in December?"

She replied,"It went up to 400 percent. I ended the year with the best sales record in the city. This was in spite of the fact that I was given the worst section in the city as my territory, the blighted area of the South Side."

I persisted, "What happened last year?"

"I did 125 percent of my yearly quota, ending up again top salesperson in Chicago. The other salespeople in my office wondered how I did it.

"In the afternoon it was my habit to be in my office. As soon as I sat down at my desk, phone calls would come from persons who wished to place their orders with me. Yet in the morning the phone on my desk was silent."

I thought a moment and said, "If your company does not recognize the extraordinary person that you really are, see me; I'll find you a better job."

A few days later, Ann phoned me, "What did you do to me? My company made me a supervisor! I now have 7 salespersons working for me." Of course I did nothing to her. She did it all herself. Oh yes, we ordered a typewriter from her.

SOARING LIKE A ROCKET

On occasion I have used visualization to help another

person's business. I often go swimming at a local YMCA pool. One day I paused in my swim and looked up at the life guard. Knowing the man was a part-time life guard, I asked, "Eric, what kind of work do you do?" He replied that he was in air conditioning. "How's business?" I asked. With a shrug of his shoulders he replied that it could be a lot better. I smiled and asked a foolish question, "Want more business?" Seeing him nod his head, I closed my eyes and visualized him being very pleased with all the work he was getting. I promptly dismissed the thought from my mind and returned to my swim.

A week passed and again I asked Eric how business was. He looked at me with a puzzled expression. "I'm glad you asked. In the past I would quote 30 or more jobs and get about three. Last week I got every one!" As I questioned him further, Eric revealed that he performed another specialty which was very profitable. My eyes again closed. Two weeks later he informed me that two of the profitable jobs came in. I shot back, "You have one more coming!" On the following month Eric's business was also great. I handed him a copy of the first edition of this book with the advice, "Read this, you can learn to do what I do."

Six months later Eric went out of business. It was obvious to me that he had assumed that his increase in business was due to coincidence or good luck. More than likely he had not read the book. Rockets do return to earth.

As we gain experience in using our mind to

successfully control what happens to us, we become more confident in our ability to solve problems. The examples in the next chapter are cases which at first appeared to have no solutions, yet were all satisfactorily resolved.

CHAPTER 4

STANDING TALL

PEACE PILGRIM, TEACHER

The inspiration for this book was my friend, the mystic Peace Pilgrim. She was a person who traveled throughout the country speaking about peace among nations, peace among people and peace within. She often spoke on the radio and television. She was the guest speaker at some the most prestigious churches and institutions in the country.

What was unusual about Peace was that she had no money, nor need for it. Her total possessions were a pen, a comb and a toothbrush. She traveled with only the clothes that she wore. She never failed in the 25 years of pilgrimage to be on time for her talk, yet she had no reliable means of transportation. It appeared to me that whatever she needed would become available to her within minutes. Let me illustrate this.

During a visit to my office Peace asked if I had small envelopes for the some 50 letters she wrote each week. I shook my head as I did not know where they could be found, even if we had them. "What about in that drawer?" she asked, pointing to it. I opened the drawer and to my surprise, it yielded the exact size of envelopes!

On another occasion at my home she asked if I had a manual typewriter. All of her letters were written on such a machine. "No", I replied, "I only have this electric typewriter here." I reached over to the machine and pulled off its cover. I could not believe what I saw; the machine was a manual typewriter! There was a new ribbon on it and it was in perfect condition. Where it came from was a mystery to me. It was quite likely that I had prepared it in anticipation of her visit but I don't recall doing so.

She liked to type outdoors and frequently needed a cardtable. At my office she asked me if I had one. "I don't believe so," I replied and then dismissed the request from my mind. A short while later, she was happily typing away on a manual typewriter sitting on top of a cardtable!

The next time she asked for a card table I was quick to respond, "I know of no cardtable in this house, but there's one around here somewhere."

She pointed to a stack of folding end tables, "What can be done with those?" she asked.

Fifteen minutes later with the use of four clamps and some ingenuity, she had a perfect cardtable!

It was a few weeks before her fatal automobile accident that I asked her, "Peace, do you always get what you need?" She replied, "Gene, even before I know that I need it, it is there before me."

Seeing an example is an excellent way to learn, second only to doing something yourself. The daily little miracles Peace was performing before my very eyes were the inspiration for me to seek the knowledge that would some day enable me to do the same. Throughout my years of study, I have acquired some of that knowledge, but I cannot compare myself with Peace, the master, who lived completely within the Law.

COLLECT EGGCUPS

You ask, "Yes, perhaps you can produce what you need in your life, but no matter how positive I try to be, I am always broke." Or: "I tried your methods to help my financial problem, yet I'm always in debt." This type of complaint is often heard.

The solution to such a problem comes in three parts. To begin with, you should start with something small and easy to believe, things that you can readily accept. Avoid trying to win instant millions in the lottery. This is difficult to believe. You may be able to do that sort of thing later.

You may start, for instance, wanting information on something that interests you. Think this way: know that it will be forthcoming, say in three days. Then dismiss the thought. The information will come to you. It may come from a book you happened to pick up, from a chance conversation or from an inspirational thought.

You may desire to acquire an unusually object. For example, not long ago I wanted to buy eggcups yet none of the clerks in the department stores I visited had even heard of eggcups. After many futile inquiries, I gave up hunting for them and dismissed the matter from my mind. A few days later I went to a flea market. I stopped at a booth with a motley collection of chinaware. With a positive thought, I spoke to the saleslady. "You have an eggcup somewhere, let's see it."

"Oh yes," she replied, "here it is."

I had my eggcup and from then on wherever I went I seemed to acquire eggcups. I now have quite a collection of them. Don't ask for a great deal at first. Be content to begin with small things such as an eggcup. Bigger and more important things will come later.

The second secret for making your thoughts work for you is belief. You must train your mind to accept the belief that something good will happen to you. All too often we use our belief to accept an idea that something of a negative nature will occur, and it does. Since most of us have had ample proof that a negative belief does influence the disasters which have befallen us, is it not logical then to turn that belief around to produce only good experiences? This is not easy at first. Remember, though, that when you experience your first success in locating one eggcup, many eggcups will surely follow.

The third part of successfully using your mind is the easiest. Be yourself; go about your business in your normal way. Be active, the opportunities will present themselves and you will recognize them. It goes without saying, however, that should you be a recluse and have no dealings with the world about you, your baitless hook will catch few fish.

QUANTUM JUMP

At times in our lives we are faced with what appear to be insurmountable problems. I can recall that when I was a child, some problems seemed crushing. My brother and I had gone to the beach, leaving our clothing in unlocked lockers. On returning to my locker I found all my clothes gone. How were we to go home when I had but my swimming trunks on? (My brother shared his clothing with me and both half dressed we made it home.) On another occasion, I had skipped school one day once too often which resulted in my flunking one test after another. Would the teacher pass me on to the next grade? (No, I stayed in her class for another semester.) As a preschooler of five, I accompanied my older brother, age six, and his friends to White City, the famous amusement park. Our banker, age 7, without foresight spent our last nickel on candy, leaving us without carfare to go home. How were we to go home, a distance of 5 miles? Yes, we somehow made it after catching a lumber wagon pulled by two horses and chased by a private policeman who caught us swiping corn from a farmer's field. These were real problems then, yet somehow I survived them. Today, as adults we look back at such problems perhaps with amusement as they don't compare with our present day almost overwhelming situations.

Let us reflect upon the big problems that we have solved. We all can recall situations that placed us in awkward, often stressful predicaments. Yet, as we look back at them, we take pride in the fact that we did come up with the successful solution to the problem. In fact, upon reflection we admit that we learned a great deal from what was then a most unhappy experience. A truth emerges here. *The greater the problem that we encounter and solve the more we learn.* Also, all other problems that we have solved in the past will appear to be of lesser significance.

Peace Pilgrim said, "We are never given a problem that we cannot solve. The more difficult the problem that is given to us, the greater our opportunity for spiritual growth." Sometimes we are given a problem that appears to have no solution, one that is certain to lead to dire consequences. During WW II as a forward artillery observer I found myself in some very unpleasant situations. Let me tell one that almost killed me.

YOU CAN IF YOU THINK YOU CAN

In the final battle in Normandy my men and I manned a radio relay station located on top of the highest hill on the front line. The hill, known as "Bloody Hill", was the prime target for a long range enemy gun. Every 5 to 10 minutes a large calibre shell would streak in upon us and explode, often but a few yards from our foxhole. The direction of the gun was not too difficult to determined but the distance was so great that the gun could not be heard or seen. For hours dozens of shells poured down on us. What was to be done? This was the climax of 12 days of battle. I was exhausted, yet this was an urgent situation; I had to think calmly and clearly. How could I stop that gun from firing? I couldn't see it; *they could see me* . This was the key to the solution.

I requested a spotter plane to fly well back of our hill where it could be seen by the enemy forward artillery observer but could not be touched by antiaircraft guns. I was confident that the gun would cease firing for fear of discovery by the observation plane. When the plane appeared above us, as anticipated, the gun stopped firing. It was silent for the duration of the battle.

A SQUEEZE ON THE POCKETBOOK

The financial world can also be a battleground as illustrated in the following account.

Some years ago I was involved in a no-win financial tangle. A partner and I had purchased 4 residential lots in a promising suburban area. A substantial mortgage was procured from a savings and loan association. Shortly after the purchase, a recession hit the country and the first to feel the blow was real estate. A few months later the savings & loan failed and was taken over by a larger S & L. For a short time we were delinquent in paying the mortgage installments. When we tried to resume payments, the second institution, also being in financial trouble, refused to negotiate the issue. In fact, they began foreclosure proceedings. By this time we were in the unfortunate position of losing well over a hundred thousand dollars, as the lots when sold in the depressed market would bring but a fraction of their original cost.

The attorney for the second S & L would not compromise; he insisted on proceeding with the foreclosure. My partner was broke. I had property and after the fore-closure the S & L would certainly first look to me to collect the outstanding note on the residential lots. I was worried. What were we to do? Then I began to think.

If I really believed in the power of the mind then surely this problem could be solved. On the day before the foreclosure date I sat down in my chair, quieted my mind and then pictured everyone involved, the attorneys, my partner and myself, perfectly pleased with the outcome of the proceedings. I felt confident that the results would be for the best interest of all concerned. I then released the entire problem to the Superconscious.

Two hours later our attorney phoned me and said he had a deal. The foreclosure would be cancelled if a $5000 payment was made to the S & L and the mortgage payments resumed. The money was paid.

A short time later the second S & L went under and the assets were purchased by a third S & L.

The third savings institution would accept no payments. Apparently all records were lost or mislaid. Three years later they began foreclosure proceedings. When they were reminded of the agreement made with the second S & L and the deposit made, it was discovered that no record was ever made of this agreement nor of the $5000 having been received. It was the tip off that the attorney for the second S & L had pocketed our $5000. After that discovery we quickly reached an agreement that was acceptable to all parties.

My mental programming in visualizing everyone pleased with the outcome of the situation took an unanticipated twist. The person who was most pleased was certainly the lawyer of the second S & L who had lifted the $5000! I should add that our problems brought to light the discovery that he had actually absconded with over $200,000 of the second S & L money.

Since then I have encountered many difficult situations but when I compare them with the harrowing experience on the hill, and the threatened foreclosure on the four lots, I never have any doubt that a satisfactory solution will present itself. Also, since I had experienced the top limit of stress, few situations today are stressful to me.

As we progress in our ability to use our mind, we are ready for greater challenges and opportunities as illustrated in the following chapter.

CHAPTER 5

TURNING MISFORTUNES INTO OPPORTUNITIES

GETTING A JOB DONE

Some years ago I was being driven by a young man on an expressway. We ran out of gas and were forced to pull off to the side of the road. I exclaimed, "Something good is about to happen!" The young man cocked his head sideways and gave me a questioning look. "Watch, you'll see," I said, as I opened the door to walk to the rear of the car.

Five minutes later a man in a late model car stopped behind us and asked if he could be of assistance. When I told him that we had run out of gas, he offered to take me to the nearest gas station.

On the way back to our car with a full can of gas, I asked our benefactor what type of work he did.

He replied, "I'm a painter. I paint houses."

"Great!" I exclaimed, "I've been looking for someone to paint our factory. Only last week I bought 24 gallons of paint at an auction for that purpose."

Two weeks later our factory was attractively painted. And the price was right!

CONDITIONING THE MIND

As a child of twelve, I made up my mind what I would like to accomplish in my lifetime. I said to myself, "I want to know, I want to build, I want to love and be loved."

Since that time I have made many detours. I had considered making the army a full-time career. Army life was fascinating at times, particularly when there was plenty of action. Yet, being in a peacetime army is like working for a large corporation. I decided that it was not for me. I spent 18 months as a traveling salesman on commission and went broke. I worked at three full time jobs as a manager, quit two and was sacked on the third.

On that third job, I earned the dismissal. I was asked by the owner of my company to devise an incentive plan to increase production and decrease the overall costs. Shortly afterward I came up with a plan that I thought was fair to both employees and management. I was unaware that the owner had the union in his pocket. The incentive payment was cut in half and the output requirement was increased 50 percent. The union representative accepted the revised plan and the workers were given no choice in the matter. As the factory manager, I became the fall guy as I had to implement the new, unfair program. It wasn't long before I was faced with the deep resentment of the union workers. I appealed to the owner to change the program but was ignored.

The end came for me when I blackened the eye of the union steward. In the fight that followed he plunged a knife in my back. I still carry the scar. Little did I know at the time that he had done me a great favor.

I resolved never to work for another company. My month's convalescence gave me time to think and I decided to go into my own business. Without money and heavily in debt, I felt very fortunate to obtain one-third of the funds needed to start my manufacturing business. I started the business in the basement of my apartment building. In 18 months the company made a profit of $70,000, three times the amount originally projected! At the age of 36, my childhood dream was coming into reality.

THE GIANT KILLER

Several years ago with General Motors engineers our company developed a special product used in a critical application on a new locomotive. After six years of development, a small production order was placed with our company with an admonition from the buyer that we should be prepared to supply at least 500 units in the next 12 months. Shortly afterwards we delivered the initial order and placed orders for parts and tools for the anticipated yearly requirement.

Six months passed and no further orders for the parts were placed with us. I called on the buyer.

"Sorry, Mr. Maurey," he explained, "we were able to get the part cheaper from a second source. We are now buying all our requirement from them."

I reminded the buyer that he had said that I should expect an order for 500 units and should be prepared to make on-time deliveries.

"Yes," he admitted, "that is so, but I am unable to do anything about it."

I thought a moment and smiled, "There is a moral problem here." He agreed. I asked, "Who is your immediate supervisor?" I was directed to the Purchasing Agent.

All documents were sent to the Purchasing Agent who shortly afterwards asked me to call on him.

"Mr. Maurey," he said, "I reviewed the file and find nothing out of order. We can do nothing for you."

I agreed that the paperwork was correct but reminded him of what his buyer had said. I concluded with the statement, "There is a moral problem involved here." I then asked for the name of the Director of Purchasing. Correspondence was again forwarded.

It was the same song with the director. I then asked for the name of the General Manager. I sent the now considerable correspondence to him.

Two weeks later I was asked to call on the Director of Purchasing. Gathered in his office at the appointed time was the original buyer, the Purchasing Agent, the Engineering Director, the project engineer and all other persons who had been involved.

The Works Manager walked in and listened to my story which brought to light the moral problem. As he walked out he said, "Take care of Mr. Maurey."

All parts on hand were purchased by General Motors and harmony between our companies was maintained. Later it developed that the second source units failed in the field and had to be 100% replaced by the Maurey product!

Although our company had no legal recourse, I knew that if I kept my cool and held firm to the belief that all would turn out well, the results would be satisfactory. We are now a major supplier for the General Motors locomotives.

The mystic, Peace Pilgrim, said, "When you see strife, see in your heart only harmony. The anger will subside, the fighting will stop."

THE STUFF DREAMS ARE MADE OF

When I was very young I was fortunate enough to know what direction I wanted my life to take. I am a factory owner. My father was a factory owner in this country and his father managed a factory in Alsace, France. When I was a youngster it wasn't difficult for me to visualize myself owning a factory. This is rarely the situation for the vast number of young people first entering our workforce. All too often, they have no idea whatsoever what they want to do with their lives.

I take every opportunity to talk with young people about the direction they are taking in their lives. I often ask such a person three questions. The first is, "What do you want to be and do five years from now?" The usually answer is that he would like to be in his present job making more money. Questioning him further, I suggest that perhaps he would also like to learn a trade, perhaps get more education. I suggest that there are many opportunities to advance his education. Would he like to marry, have children and feel financially secure? This starts him thinking about his future.

My second question follows, "What do you want to be 10 years from now?" Now the person begins to really think and will reply. "Yes, I want everything mentioned, plus more of the same." With further questioning and suggestions the person begins to see himself more secure and sure of himself. He starts to feel a direction.

My third question is the clincher. "What do you want to *feel* and be 20 years from now?" Often a young man will say. "I want to be retired on a pension." I then remind him that he will be about 40 and will then have at least another 30 to 40 years to live and be productive. I suggest to him that possibly he would like to enjoy good health at that age, that he would like to be a respected person in the community. I ply him with other suggestions that will get him to think about his future. Starting at that moment, he cannot avoid making long-range plans.

It is predictable what will happen. Once a person has put into his/her subconscious mind a direction to follow, the Power that is touched will propel him/her there. Rev. Gerald Loe says it in a back-handed way. "You create your own reality. Everyone who finds himself in a spot created it for himself."

GETTING THERE

Some years ago I became acquainted with a young lady from Germany who was a professional accountant. After two years of frustration in her job and personal life she decided to return to Europe. Shortly before she left I asked her a question.

"Heide," I said, "If I could wave a magic wand over you and grant your every wish, what situation would you like to find yourself in five years from now?"

She thought a moment and replied. "I would like to be married to someone in this country who has a similar profession to mine. She paused and added, "and have two children."

Unlike most young persons, Heide knew exactly what she wanted and she had the courage to go after it. Soon after leaving for Europe, she made a sudden return to this country. In a few years she was happily married to an accountant and it wasn't long afterwards that they had two children.

People who have a positive outlook on life, such as Heide, are well on the way to experiencing success in many areas of their lives. With this positive attitude in mind we shall examine in the next chapter a practical method of attaining prosperity, a goal many eagerly seek.

CHAPTER 6

HOW TO BECOME RICH

WHERE IS YOUR ATTENTION?

Before venturing on the road to becoming wealthy, let me tell you how to lose your shirt in the attempt to become rich. The best way to do this is to divide your attention. Let me illustrate.

Some years back I decided that one of the ways to expand my business was to purchase other companies and become a director of multiple businesses. Shortly afterwards opportunities were offered me and I purchased two promising companies whose products were unrelated to what my company produced. I had immediately made two mistakes. First, I had little technical knowledge of the processes of either company and second, both companies were at a distance from the parent company.

My concentration was now focused in three directions. Any company or new venture needs considerable attention at first. Attaining success is a full time job. Although I had appointed managers for the two new companies, I could not give enough personal attention to each company. It wasn't long before both began to drain my energy and resources. Within a year, after a considerable financial loss, I chucked both of them out of my corporate structure. What was even more serious, the parent company also suffered a substantial loss.

What had really , happened? I had divided my attention in too many directions. I learned the truth the hard way. *Whatever you give your attention to, this is where you will have your success.*

How often have you experienced this law with regret? Have you started a part-time business or moonlight operation and found that it resulted in wasted effort and very little compensation? More than likely you have also found that the excursion in another direction hurt your progress in your main occupation.

If you want to be successful in your business or profession, give your full attention to it. Part time work will never get you off the ground.

Conclusion: It is impossible to love two women at the same time. Give your attention to one and you have a good chance of success.

WHAT IS TIME?

A number of times we have asked you to keep everything in the present. There is a purpose in this. Before further discussion, let us examine what is time. Time is a manmade invention. Let us see how this came about.

Long ago, it was observed by astronomers (known as astrologers then) that the seasons progressed and the position of the stars changed in a 365 day cycle. (Later that was corrected to 365 1/4 days when leap year was added.) The early astrologers noted that the heavens could conveniently be divided into 12 parts. These parts were subsequently called the Signs of the Zodiac.

In an area in England, rising up from the plains, there are peculiarly shaped hills about one hundred feet high and some as long as a thousand feet. This obvious abnormality could not be explained until recent times. In 1955 an airplane pilot looking down over this area suddenly saw the answer to the riddle. It was the symbol of the Zodiac, 22 miles in diameter, with the town of Butleigh as its center. Apparently a prehistoric group of astrologers had arranged the hills in the exact position of the stars they saw that represented to them the position of the 13 parts of the Zodiac symbols. (The movement of the stars relative to each other since that time has resulted in our seeing but 12 parts today.)

These ancient people were able to mark their time of existence accurately on the ground. Perhaps they were the builders of England's Stonehenge (a group of hugh stones placed in a circle), probably contemporaneous with the astrologers of Babylon. We are now finding out that the ancients were smarter than we have been given to think.

Time is a minor problem to the present day astronomer. With the planetarium machine he can turn back the heavens placing the stars back in their former position thousands of years ago. In a sense the astronomer turns back time and can live at the time when the hills were constructed!

THE ENIGMA OF TIME

The National Geographic, Vol.177, No.3, March 1990 talks about the complexity of describing time. "We have given more attention to measuring time than to anything in nature, "says Gernot Winkler, Director of Time Services at the U.S. Naval Observatory in Washington, D.C. "But time remains an abstraction, a riddle that exists only in our minds."

"Psychologists tells us that children before the age of two have little sense of the passage of time. It may have been the same for our early ancestors. Some scholars believe that people once lived in a state of "timeless present" with little or no sense of past or future.

"Julian Jaynes, a Princeton psychologist and author, contends this may have been true as late as the eighth century B.C., when the *Iliad* was first written down. He observes that the epic poem attributed to Homer displays little awareness of time.

"According to Jaynes the poem was about people who ` did not live in a frame of past happenings, who did not have *lifetimes* in our sense, and who could not reminisce.' -

abilities that were acquired only when language advanced to the point that the past could be described in terms of personal experience."

During this century science has changed its concept of time. Throughout recorded history time was looked upon as flowing like a river. The English scientist Sir Isaac Newton held that time compared to lilies flowing downstream in absolute order, with no end to lilies. Albert Einstein's theories of relativity brought a new concept to time. He saw time as a dimension - like height and width - giving meaning to events and the order in which they occur. To him it was useful in keeping everything from happening all at one time.

Einstein further proved that our perception of time is distinctive only to our planet. This is because time is affected by the unique gravitational field of each celestial body, and therefore is different at each place in the universe.

In metaphysical thinking there is no consciousness of time; no past, no future, only *now*. Let me illustrate this concept using a scientific truth. There is a star, Arcturus, 40 light years away from our solar system. This means that it takes 40 years for light to travel from the star to the earth and conversely, 40 years for earth light to reach that star. Observing Arcturus, we see what happened 40 years ago on that star. It appears to you that what you are seeing has nothing to do with time. The event occurred 40 years ago, yet in your reality it is occurring now.

Now, let us imagine that I am on Arcturus and that you can see me. If my present earth age is 60, you would see me as I was 40 years ago at age 20, since my image took 40 years to come to you. As you observe me move about on that star there would be no doubt in your mind that I am 20 years old.

Let us dream up another nonscientific, improbability. Let us assume that I am on star EM500, 500 light years away - it takes 500 years for an image to travel to earth -and you can again observe me at age 20. How old would I be today?

Shall we indulge in another gross improbability? Let us assume that you had the ability to instantaneously travel to any and every point between earth and star EM500. Is it not conceivable that you could see every event occurring in the last 500 years on star EM500 all at one time?

Let us further examine a concept that time does not exist, that there is no past nor future, only the present, the now time.

In the spirit world it is said that time does not exist. Souls who communicate through a medium often relate events they experience in sequence but they display little awareness of when it occurred. Such spirit people often speak as if they are still living in centuries long past yet they believe it is the now time. In their world should they desire to meet a person or be at a certain place, the event occurs instantaneously. There is no duration of time, no delay.

In the living world we can also experience the same process where there is no delay, no duration of time. What comes into being is instantaneous. If we can assume that time does not exist, then what we desire should be instantly available. For example, time had stopped when the vehicles were whisked from harm's way as described earlier in this book. In each case there was an urgent desire to avoid an accident without a moments delay, resulting in a traversal of the distance described in less than a split second. In our thinking, therefore, we must know that what we desire will not happen tomorrow or next week, but is happening right now. If you put the manifestation of your desire into the future, that is precisely where it will stay, in the future.

As previously mentioned, for Peace Pilgrim time had nothing to do with her desires. Whatever she needed appeared before she knew that she needed it.

You may begin to understand the difficulty a seer or life reader has in fixing the time of an event in someone's life. A picture may come to him out of the past, present or in the future. As he directs his attention to a given event, there are but few measuring sticks for him to know if the event occurred in the past, is occurring or will occur.

This concept of time is not easily understood. Albert Einstein, the great physicist, grappled with it for years until he equated it to the fourth dimension in his Theory of Relativity. As a measuring stick how difficult this can be, let us assume that we have a two dimensional being, a bug swimming in a pool of placid water. Should he meet an obstacle, such as a floating ring of string around him, he cannot escape because the third dimension (up) is not part of his understanding. A miracle happens, you see the situation and carefully elevate the bug (using third dimension) and place it outside of the loop of string. The string (danger) has miraculously been avoided. Our two dimensional bug will never know what happened because height does not exist for it. He knows nothing about the third dimension.

Here is another thought on the concept of time. We know that a gasoline vehicle has thousands of explosions in its cylinders, often in minutes. Over the years that the vehicle is driven, there are millions of explosions. Billions? If all of these explosions were compressed within a split second, what would we have? Certainly a big bang! An atomic explosion?

Should there be beings from outer space who travel millions of miles to visit us, could it be possible that they have learned to overcome duration of time and travel such distances in less than a split second? If they can do it, why can't we?

In actual practice, time is not fixed in relation to events. Often when one has a strong desire, that desire comes instantly into being yet the circumstances leading up to the moment of desire occurred days or even months prior to the event. The insurance salesman in the following anecdote had just such an experience.

LAW OF SEED MONEY

What appears to be the most guarded secret system of multiplying wealth is *The Law of Seed Money*. It is the practice of giving to others part of all that is earned or accumulated. Men such as Julius Rosenwald, Andrew Carnegie and John D. Rockefeller all were aware of the Law of Seed Money and practiced it throughout their long and extremely prosperous lives. Not only did such men enrich the world by their giving but they knew how to claim the multiplied returns of their gifts.

The Law of Seed Money is to give generously and unselfishly knowing that you will receive all that you need. It is not as simple as it may seem. The trick is to convince your subconscious mind that you can give generously because you are wealthy *now*. Your subconscious then taps the Source which brings into your awareness the condition of wealth.

This process is not to be confused with tithing. A tithe is a tax of 10 percent of one's income given to maintain a religious institution. It is an obligation, not a gift.

DON'T PUT A LIMIT ON IT, GOD

There is a little booklet called *Seed Money in Action* which I frequently pass out to my friends and acquaintances. I call it the "Wealth Generator". In brief, the book spells out the steps you take in giving *knowing* that you will receive all that you need. (This small volume has been included in the bibliography in the back of this book.)

During a conversation with an insurance salesman in my office, I handed him the seed money booklet with the remark, "Read this, Bob, and give it a try."

Two weeks later a very excited Bob returned to my office exclaiming, "It works! I tried it, it works!"

He then told me about going to church on Sunday and dropping a five dollar donation into the basket with the comment, "Don't put any limit on it God!"

On the following Wednesday he was delighted to find a check in the mail for a $250 bonus. Obviously, some time prior, the check had been prepared and mailed to him. The money was his before he went to church. The time of his receiving it was determined by his strength of belief. Time had no bearing on the working of the law. He had applied the well known *Law of Seed Money*.

THE BREAKTHROUGH

When I first heard of the Law of Seed Money I was practically broke. My business owed a past due $35,000 loan to the bank and more than $50,000 to our suppliers. I had less than $2,000 in my personal account. As I didn't have much to lose I decided to use the Law.

I had to first convince my subconscious mind that I was already prosperous. To do this I began by picking up the tabs at the restaurants, leaving generous tips. I bought a new suit and even a used Cadillac car. A month passed. My checking account showed a $5000 balance! Six months later it was up to $10,000. It has increased ever since. Gradually I became convinced that the time was ripe to really put the law to the test.

IF YOU BELIEVE IT, PROVE IT!

About 10 years ago our business sales were off and there was little promise of sales increasing. I called my secretary, Betty Petrus, to my desk and announced. "We're going to give everybody a 6 percent raise."

She was aghast and exclaimed, "You can't do that Mr. Maurey, you know our cash position is low and business is down!"

When our superintendent, Leonor Ojeda, heard what I proposed to do she said, "There are not enough orders. I was about to recommend that we reduce the work week from 5 days to 4. I simply can't keep the people busy."

The comptroller, Tom Morris, was even more forceful in his resistance to my idea, "Don't you know, Mr. M., there is a recession out there? This is certainly not the time to give raises!"

To everyone I calmly replied, "We're going to give everybody a raise." And we did.

The month after the raise, business came in from all parts of the country. Our executives were pleased and surprised with the excellent increase in sales. They thought it was coincidence. Not I.

Eight months later sales started to falter. Time for another raise. Again there was the same resistance to my proposal. I turned to our superintendent, Leonor, and instructed, "Hire six more people; we will need them next month." Now everyone knew I had flipped!

The following month we broke every record for sales in the 30 year history of the company! Since that time there has never been the slightest opposition to a proposed raise. Everyone knows what to expect.

What was my thinking when I proposed the raises? I knew that if I could convince myself that the company was already prosperous and could well afford the raises, it would become prosperous. Neither time or economic conditions were factors; I held the thought that the company was prosperous *now*. Later I realize that the added money in each paycheck made the employees also feel prosperous. That feeling contributed greatly to the added prosperity of the company.

The Law of Seed Money also works in reverse. An ex-convict complained to me that when was sent to prison someone broke into his apartment and relieved him of $6000 worth of tools. He wasn't pleased when I reminded him that during his late career he had held up a tavern to the tune of $600!

Now that we know that our desires can be fulfilled by a strong belief, let us examine another tool that can be most helpful to us. The tool is another law, the Law of Attraction, the subject of the following chapter.

CHAPTER 7

LAW OF ATTRACTION

THE LAW

The Law of Attraction states that when you create a need, a source that has a corresponding desire to fulfill that need will become available to you. You have often experienced this law in a number of different ways. You have wanted something and that very thing shortly becomes available to you. You wanted to meet a particular person and soon afterward that person makes an appearance. You may call it coincidence. Not so. When you place in mind a thought which carries with it some kind of emotion, - the more feeling in it, the better - that thought orders your subconscious to produce the desired result. When the thought is released and forgotten, the subconscious goes to work. The source of all power and intelligence is contacted and shortly afterward you have your "coincidence". (See figure 1)

Mark Twain was noted for his economy of effort. When he became curious about the latest news of a distant friend, he would not write him to make inquiries. He simply knew that his friend would pick up his thoughts and would soon write to him. In a few days the expected letter would arrive!

The Law may be stated in another way. Create a vacuum and it will be quickly filled. Caution must be used to avoid thinking about those things that you don't want. Your subconscious mind cannot judge whether something is good or bad for you. Give it power and it will go right ahead and produce it for you. In this sense, your individualized subconscious can be likened to a small child. Whatever you say, the child believes and acts upon it without using judgment.

HOW TO ATTRACT A THIEF

One of the best illustrations of the power given to a negative thought is an experience that my secretary, Betty Petrus, had. One Friday evening Betty decided to carry home $1000 in cash rather than leave it in the office over the weekend.

On returning to the office on Monday morning with the cash in her handbag she felt highly apprehensive. She had but a short walk as the office was only a block away from her home. Without warning a man appeared behind her with a knife and demanded that she accompany him through the passageway between the adjacent small homes. She had the presence of mind to fall to the sidewalk, clutch her handbag and scream! The man, frightened, darted away through the passageway and disappeared.

Betty unknowingly had attracted the thief to her. She was fearful and had unconsciously radiated that message to a thief who was looking for a victim. The Law of Attraction does not discriminate between right and wrong; it always works.

HOW TO MAKE A CON-ARTIST HAPPY

A friend complained that she got ripped off by a confidence man yet she had felt that this was a person of honesty and integrity. There is a rule that the con-artist consistently follows. He seeks a victim who thinks he can get an enormous bargain, one which usually involves an element of chicanery. When a con-man can arouse a person's greed, he has a victim. Greed or the intense desire to acquire property is often a subconscious emotion not recognized by our consciousness. We learn about it all too late when disaster strikes. The victim actually attracts the undesirable situation to himself.

HOW TO GET OTHERS TO DO YOUR WORK

On a more positive note, Dr. Marcus Bach tells an unusual story. It seems that he had a huge pile of dirt he desired to move across his driveway. He began the arduous task with shovel and wheelbarrow but a short while later it began to rain. He thought, "What am I to do now? The rain will wash the dirt away." After a moment's hesitation, he decided, "I'm doing this all wrong", went into his home, sat down, closed his eyes and relaxed.

His wife asked, "What are you doing?"

He replied, "I'm moving the dirt across the drive-way!"

A few minutes later a knock came at the door. A contractor asked if he could park his bulldozer and other equipment over the weekend on an unused area of Dr. Bach's property.

"Certainly," replied Dr. Bach, and he added with a sly grin, "but would you mind moving that pile of dirt across the driveway?"

The dirt was promptly moved. This is a positive demonstration of the Law of Attraction in action.

LOVE COMES WITH A WASTEBASKET

There is a good chance that half of the people reading this book will take a crack at practicing the technique illustrated in the following anecdote as related to me by a lifelong friend, age 70. I should add that my friend could be described as a metaphysician, having practiced the art for many years.

For several years he had no one with whom to share his life. Finally, he became tired of living alone and decided to program the perfect mate for himself. He relaxed in a comfortable chair and performed a simple visualization. He saw himself being very pleased with a most loving woman; in every respect she was perfect for him. Also, he visualized her very pleased with him and perfect for her. With a wry smile he made only one precondition: that she be 35 years old! He promptly dismissed his thoughts. Five weeks later it happened.

Where did he find her? At his office under his desk!

The Polish cleanup lady was pulling the wastebasket from under his desk. He said to her,"Come up here, I want to look at you." He sized her up and said, "I've been looking for someone your size who can use some good used clothing." Taking out a measuring tape from his desk, he continued, "Let me measure you." The young lady flushed but said nothing. She spoke little English. As soon as my friend touched the lady, both knew that there was something special between them. It later developed that for a long time she had secretly admired my friend but since there was a language barrier she kept her thoughts to herself.

Yes, she was exactly 35 years old!

When my friend programs something to happen, he doesn't do things half way.

To his added delight he discovered that his young lady was a civil engineer with six years supervision experience building roads and bridges in Poland. Since she spoke no English when she came to this country, she took the first job offered, a clean up job. Often she had admired the new unused drafting table in his office: it is hers now. She works in his office as an engineer. They plan to marry.

Another coincidence: Her father is a tailor in Poland. Some 40 years ago a beautiful lady called on him for a special dress to be made. He also placed his tape measure on her. Instantly they, too, knew that this was an important beginning for them. The lady is her mother. Was this a coincident? Or was it something else?

One of my friends who previewed the manuscript for this book asked, "If a person could make a miracle happen for finding his "bliss" like that, do you have any suggestions for others on the same pursuit?" These are my thoughts:

First of all, there should be no, or at least very few, preconditions. Almost with blind fate the person must know that what comes into being is correct. It is like opening a box wrapped in old newspapers with a ragged twine and finding within a perfect diamond. How many of us throw away such a box without opening it!

Secondly, don't hang on to an intolerable condition until something better comes along. Create a vacuum in your life. Remove the chains from your life that bind you to a situation that you are fairly convinced will not improve. This takes courage, it may mean a matter of life or death. It may mean great financial cost. It will certainly mean emotional trauma. Nothing will happen until you have created the vacuum.

Out there somewhere (she, too, may be found under your desk) is someone who needs you. Allow the Law of Attraction to work for you, allow someone to be drawn into the vacuum of your heart.

Finally, know that what you have put into Mind will happen and then dismiss it from your thoughts. Let it happen to you.

Sounds simple? Yes, and it works.

TAKE A CHANCE AND WIN!

At times the Law of Attraction will not be obvious. There will be occasions when you cannot specifically predetermine what will be best for you. You are forced to make a choice. For example, you may entertain doubts about taking a course of study at an institution of learning. You are not sure that you will learn anything of value and you fear that it will be a waste of time and money. On the other hand there is a 50/50 chance that you will learn something of importance. What should you do? In truth, whatever decision that you make is the correct one. When you have confidence that the Law is working for your benefit, there is only opportunity for you. Let me illustrate.

In 1973, my daughter, Carol, said, "Dad, there is a course called *Silva Mind Control* which I think you would like. Why don't you look into it?" Knowing that I was being led in the right direction, I took the course. Over the years it has resulted in enormous benefits for me. It has brought me health, wealth and happiness.

NEGATIVE ENCOUNTERS

On the other hand, with equal confidence I took a course called *Est.* It was not a pleasant encounter. Yet not all was lost. I learned something I never expected. I discovered in myself the power to recognize and resist brainwashing, the basic technique used in the course. I now can recognize brainwashing whether it occurs in the news media, in the books I read or in the lectures that I may attend.

The brainwashing that goes on in advertising, especially in Television, can be pure scam. Take the product where the miserable creature is suffering from a headache. He takes the chemical compound and almost immediately he is smiling without pain. He should be looking instead for the cause of the headache, perhaps taking a few minutes off to relieve stress by relaxing and deep breathing. I recall one ad showing a beautiful young lady dipping her fingers in pure dish washing detergent.

She mouthed, "This soft, velvety detergent is so kind to my hands." The same detergent is so powerful that it takes the skin off my fingers. The ad was taken off the air waves.

Throughout the day we hear, see, smell, taste and touch. We are exposed to an avalanche of sights and sounds, many of which are destructive and highly negative. We must be able to distinguish between that which is the truth and good for us and the false which will surely lead us in a sorry direction.

In the next chapter we will explore another law that is acting for or against us all the time. This law when not thoroughly understood can get us in a lot of trouble, in particular when we talk too much.

CHAPTER 8

LAW OF COMMUNICATION

CAN YOU KEEP A SECRET?

The next law to be discussed can cause you a lot of trouble when you don't understand it. It is called the *Law of Communication*. It simply means that *everything you think of and do becomes public property in the Superconscious or Universal Mind.* When you have solved a problem and come up with an original idea, that idea may be picked up anywhere in the world by someone seeking an answer to a similar problem. This process is analogous to data being fed into a computer and being accessed by unknown persons. You may ask the question then, "Was it my idea in the first place?"

Because of this inexhaustible pipeline of information, the airplane was simultaneously invented in the United States, Russia and France. Almost to the day, the inventors in each country flew their first airplane, completely unaware of the others.

Charles Darwin was not the first to conceive the theory accredited to him, the Theory of Evolution. Another man had the same idea before he did. But the two men did not know each other. Just recently it was brought out (U & lc, a type designer's publication) that Johann Gutenberg did not invent the printing press. He did invent many things relating to printing, but not the press. And he did not know the man who did.

NEVER TELL A RAT A SECRET!

The scientific community is now on the threshold of proving the *Law of Communication*. In experiments performed by Dr. W. Shelldrake in which he taught rats to go through a test maze, he found that it took the rats a given length of instruction time to learn to travel through the maze. Succeeding generations of rats took a shorter time to learn the same task. What was not anticipated, however, was that rats in another part of the world, in no way linked to Shelldrake's rats, would also exhibit this same shortened interval of time on an identical test maze.

CAPITALIZE ON YOUR IDEAS!

When you have what you think is an original idea, do not discuss it with just anyone. Look to the *Law of Communication* to attract all that you will need to bring your idea to fulfillment. For example, if you have invented a useful gadget, yet need additional information and guidance to finance it, to manufacture it and to market it, lean on this law to supply the answers. Ideas and interested persons will be drawn to you. Do not discuss all problems of your project with these people, but only those parts which specifically pertain to their specialty. You must look for a positive response from each contributor, avoiding areas which do not concern them. Their inability to understand all the parts of your project can cause doubt, resulting in negative thinking. Remember, the negative thoughts of others can produce results also.

Did you ever have a good idea which went down the drain? How did this happen? A good bet is that you enthusiastically talked about it to anyone who would listen. You spoke to that sympathetic friend who nodded his head in agreement with your idea but thought, "Too bad he doesn't know all the technical problems he's getting into." You spoke to another acquaintance and he highly questioned your ability to get the project financed. You spoke to your wife about your great idea which would certainly make you both rich. She thought, "Just another one of his brainstorms!" Three strikes and you are out. And you didn't even know it. A year later you see your product in a full page ad by a company you never heard of.

The next time you get a good idea keep your mouth shut.

A DIAMOND MINE

Communication between individuals is a continuous process. Many ideas pass between people, often original, yet such ideas are ignored because people are not paying attention to what is being said.

For any business to survive, there is a constant

need for new products to be produced and/or sold. My business is no exception. For years I inquired of my sales representatives and salesmen for ideas of new products that we could develop and sell. In 37 years in business I cannot remember a single useful suggestion being advanced by them. And yet if I had been listening to another source there would have been acres of diamonds for my taking.

During the pass few years I discovered a rich source for new products. All through the years our customers and potential customers have been pointing us in the right direction but we have not been listening to them. Many engineers and scientists have contacted our company to build exotic and state-of-the-art products for them. Many of these were built and as a result we learned from them. Of course, many of the ideas were not feasible or beyond our capabilities. Our awaken concept now is to ask ourselves the key question: Is the item being requested a product that can be used by others and if we develop it can we market it and sell it for a profit? We are at long last busily picking up our diamonds.

THE THINKING MAN

About 20 years ago, John Ruzzier, a young engineer just starting in business with $400 capital and renting a section of our factory, came to me with a metal box in his hands. "What's this, Mr. Maurey?" he inquired.

I replied, "This is an instrument that we submitted to a company that wanted a solid state timing device. Our engineers built this mechanical one which was rejected."

"Do you mind if I contact the company to see if I can make one for them?" he asked.

"Not all," I replied, "Take the box and see what you can do."

Not long afterwards John developed a successful design for the customer and in a few months was producing the instrument for them. It was the start of a million dollar business.

John began to think. If a solid state timer could be sold to one customer, why not to others? John launched his company on making solid state timers. Soon John's company moved from my facility into a small store front. A year later his company rented the store next door. After other moves, always into larger facilities, his company acquired a large factory building.

John went on to develop the french fried timers used in Burger King, MacDonnells, and other fast food franchises. 16 years after John started into business, he sold the business for $4,000,000!

We have explored how this mystery works and have a good idea how we can use it. We have a fair understanding of the three parts of the mind and how each part works. We are disciplining our subconscious mind and putting it to work for us. We have explored time and conclude that we should ignore it. We liked the Law of Attraction and are wary of the Law of Communication. Now, let us get into a law that we can't mess up but only do good when using it for ourselves and for others. It's called the Law of Harmony.

CHAPTER 9

LAW OF HARMONY

HARMONY, THE LAW OF LOVE

One of the seemingly miraculous laws is the *Law of Harmony*. Simply stated: *Harmonious thought will create a corresponding harmonious condition in any given situation.*

There is creative good in everything. No matter what the circumstances may appear to be, only good can come into being when this law is applied. Let me illustrate how the Law works.

LOVE, THE SHIELD

The law may also be called the Law of Love. Peace Pilgrim told about an incident in which a man was about to commit grievous physical harm to his step-daughter. Before the man could strike the girl, Peace stepped in between them with only love in her heart for both of them. The man hesitated, looked at Peace with inquiring eyes, turned and went his way.

Harmony can be created for others by the projection of your thoughts. I have had much success in bringing about reconciliations between individuals. Most I had never met and were thousands of miles from me. To create harmony in a person's life, I use the following affirmation:

"I visualize you in a circle of your friends, family, relatives and close associates. There is joy and gladness in your hearts; smiles on your faces. There is a deep understanding of each other. Each feels love, trust, respect and forgiveness for the others. There is an all prevailing feeling of harmony within this wonderful group of people. All are thankful and grateful."

Our defense (war) industries can only exist when there is distrust, hate and fear. Intensify these emotions within the citizenry and more money is appropriated to such industries. Diminish or remove such feelings and financial support is withdrawn. What is the opposite of hate? Yes, you have it. It is love. Love is the tool that brings reconciliation, friendship, and cooperation within a society and among nations. We don't have far to look where such thinking is suppressed. Within a number of Central and South American nations there is obvious exploitation of people for power and wealth. Put love to work and dictators fall.

WANT TO STOP A WAR?

The Law of Harmony is so powerful that when it is applied, even unknowingly, conflict can be turned into tranquility and peace. My experience in Normandy during World War II is an interesting example.

On July 6, 1944, when the American army was slugging its way southward in its breakout from the Normandy peninsula in France, the German army was making a last ditch stand with the full power of its armor and guns. On that day I was determined to lay a telephone line right up to the front line to use for forward artillery observation.

I threaded my way toward the front dodging mortar and artillery shells and the occasional small arms fire directed my way.The shriek of the incoming shells and explosions shattered my nerves: I was scared. With dogged determination I plunged on until I came to the end of the wire on my reel. I spliced in the phone and cranked the call signal. The line was dead, more than likely hit by a shell that fell behind me. There was nothing more that I could do.

"Well," I thought, "The chance of living through this day is slim, but damn it, I'm going to read those letters from my wife before anything happens to me!"

With that resolve I planted my back against a hedgerow and reached inside my shirt for six unopened letters. I tore open the first letter and started reading. As the time passed with the reading of each letter, my fears vanished; I laughed aloud over the amusing contents. I completely forgot where I was.

When I put down the sixth letter, I looked around

me perplexed. There wasn't a sound to be heard! When the first letter had been opened, 30,000 men were locked in desperate combat. What had happened? Never before had I experienced so complete a silence on a battlefield. Later, we discovered that the enemy had pulled their troops out and would be on the run all the way to the borders of Germany.

On two later occasions the battle stopped just as I arrived at a front line where minutes before the fighting had been fierce. Several times infantrymen told me that they felt safe when I was present.

Today I ask myself, "Is it possible that the hedge-row where I sat had become the center of Harmony that radiated outward and touched every soldier on both sides? Or was it a coincidence?"

I have consciously used the Law of Harmony thousands of times. For me it has been consistently effective. It is highly probable that the Law was used on that Normandy battlefield.

FRIEND OR ENEMY?

Attracting friends seems to be most difficult for many people. We all know persons who complain of loneliness and of not having friends. Such persons are often referred to as "loners". When we meet such people we unconsciously back away from further relationship with them. Why? There are two basic elements: they really don't like people and they don't like themselves.

Liking yourself is not easily accomplished. You can look back at all your failures, all your regrets, all the "ifs" in your life and come up with a pretty dismal picture. Concentrating on the negative aspects of your life will certainly give you a woeful image of yourself and a resulting negative opinion of about everyone you meet. The first task in making friends is to change what you think of yourself, to concentrate on the positive aspects and experiences of your life. If you desire a change in your life, this is not an easy task. Best that you begin in a small way.

Each day there will be something good that you can do. It may be a small thing such as helping a foreign person to understand a particularly difficult word. It may be walking a few steps to thank another. It may be sharing a newspaper with a stranger. It may be picking a scrap of paper off the street and tossing it into a waste container. Throughout the day there are countless opportunities to assist others in little ways. These may not be of the utmost importance but somehow they make you feel good. Your self-image is on the way to improvement.

Later you can graduate to bigger things. You may stop to help a disable motorist. There is always an opportunity to stuff a dollar in a Salvation Army can. (This should not only make you feel good but rich as well.) You may have an opportunity to take a blind person to church. We all have special gifts to share with others. Sharing gives us a good feeling about ourselves. Give of yourself and you will feel on top of the world.

Before we can like people we must first like ourselves. I would go further; before you can fully love others you must love yourself. In this context, love is not defined as an emotion, but as a state of mind. It is an awareness of who you are, equanimity in facing life's problems and strength in stressful situations. It is non-harmful and non-selfish. It is a willingness to give of yourself, to put the other person's needs before those of yourself. At the extreme, it is giving your life to save the life of a stranger.

In a broader sense, Love is the greatest power that man can use. It is the one power that can never harm. It lifts man from the ghettos of his thinking and pressures of his environment. It determines the form of government that we have. It is found in our courts, in our church and in our hospitals. It determines whether or not there will be war or peace. It doe not discriminate; good or bad are treated impartially. In essence, Humanity will only exist as long as man cares about his fellow man.

Enid Hoffman, author, teacher of metaphysics, psychic skills and Huna, the ancient Polynesian religion, refers to herself as a "delightful person". And everyone she meets agrees with her. The little lady in her eighties attracts a host of friends who cannot do enough for her. She in turn takes every opportunity to help others with all the resources that she has. She likes herself and she likes people. She has a host of friends.

I like people, (I also think I'm a nice guy) and I have a long Christmas list. I also know something else, a little secret. I am aware that everybody I meet knows subconsciously what I am thinking. A person I meet for the first time instantly picks up my impression of them. Such people rarely know why they react to me as they do. What are my thoughts at that moment? They are always positive about the person. I like him and I am aware that he knows it. Somebody said, "To have a friend, be a friend."

We know that the mind is a wonderful and useful instrument. Let's look now at far-out skills that the mind has. Why not a miracle every now and then? You are capable of it, you know. The final chapter throws a few challenges your way.

CHAPTER 10

LET YOUR MIND BLAST OFF

THE ART OF HEALING

To those persons who have practiced reaching the seat of Power, the Superconscious Mind, spiritual or psychic healing becomes almost an everyday expectation.

The secret of spiritual healing is to concentrate directing the Healing Power to the patient. The healer's concentration is aided by visualizing a shaft of white light being directed to the patient. The white light is equated to the power of healing flowing from the Source, not from the healer. Usually, after less than a minute the healer's concentration will drift into another subject other than the task at hand. This indicates that the healer's mind was definitely in the subconscious, the communication link with the Superconscious. Since Infinite Power was tapped, even for just a second, the healing is done.

It is not necessary for the healer to have a medical knowledge of the condition of his patient. Leave it up to Infinite Intelligence where all knowledge of the patient resides. Let me illustrate this with a recent case.

UP AND RUNNING AGAIN

A friend asked me if I would send healing to her 15 year old nephew in a hospital in Poland. The details of his illness were sketchy at best. Apparently the young man had developed an illness in his head which had thrown him into a coma. The doctors were at a loss to know how to treat him. Of course I agreed to try to help.

Here is what happened. I closed my eyes and concentrated on a healing white light being directed at the young man. In about a minute I could no longer hold my attention on the white light and my mind slipped away into another subject. As soon as I realized this, I knew that the healing was done. Within two weeks the nephew returned home and is now enjoying perfect health.

The healer has nothing to do with the success or failure of his efforts. He controls nothing. In essence he is but an interested bystander with a desire to be helpful. It is practicing love in a broader sense. He understands that the Infinite Intelligence and Power that he tapped is aware of everything that is wrong with the patient. It makes the decisions.

HEAL YOURSELF

Before I became knowledgeable in the art of spiritual healing it took but one personal healing to startle me in believing that something had happened. My wife and I went to the Philippines to visit the Psychic Surgeons. These are persons who have developed a technique for opening the body with bare hands and are able to remove diseased tissue. For us westerners such a feat is hard to believe unless we see it with our own eyes. See bibliography, *Wonder Healers of the Philippines* by Harold Sherman.

While I was viewing such an operation, the healer Mercado asked if he could be of service to me.

"Possibly," I replied, "I have a sore leg. If you know of a simple method to heal it, I would pleased if you would do so." Actually, I had a severe case of sciatica in my right leg which had been with me for over two years.

"Lie down on this bed and relax." Mercado ordered. When I had complied, the healer simply passed his hands over my leg a few times. I stood up. The pain had gone! At the time it was a miracle to me.

A few years later, sciatica pain entered my left leg. By this time I knew that *all disease has a mental cause. Find it and you are healed.* Since the affliction was in the lower part of my body, I suspected that the cause was related to something unpleasant in my life, possibly a smoldering resentment or negative program hidden deep in my subconscious memory. I resolved to find the cause.

I instructed my subconscious mind to make known to me within three days the cause of the sciatica. My subconscious would have to dredge it up from where it was hidden. Gradually the truth came into my consciousness. Thirty years previously my brother, Joe, and I had a disagreement which had grievously upset both of us at the time. Over the years we had dismissed the incident from our minds and would see each other occasionally when our families had a social meeting.

Knowing that the sore leg was a blessing in disguise, I decided to do something about the unacceptable situation. A Unity treatment that I had used in the past would do the trick. I relaxed and recited aloud:

"Joe, I forgive you and let you go to your good. All is finished between us now and forever.

"Joe, you forgive me and let me go to my good. All is finished between us now and forever."

At the conclusion of the treatment I knew that our relationship was healed, not only for me but for Joe also. Since that moment we have been the best of friends, seeing each other as often as we can.

Two weeks later the sciatica left. I know it will never return.

I should add that even though the person who did you a disservice is dead, the same rule applies: your continued grievance whether it be conscious to you or not, will cause a physical disharmony in your body. Search for that episode in your life and defuse it, perhaps using the method described above. *Order* your subconscious to give you the information needed. It will come up with the answer.

The noted spiritual healer, Gerald Loe of Maywood, Illinois told of a self healing that he experienced. In 1945 he observed a lump on his left wrist, diagnosed as a cyst. A doctor removed it but three years later it again appeared. He used autosuggestion to help retard further growth, without much success. As the months passed the cyst worsened with no relief from pain.

Finally, he became angry with himself and exclaimed, "Damn it! I don't have to put up with this problem. I want this properly taken care of!" He then visualized moving his wrist perfectly in every direction without pain or a lump. He promptly forgot about it. A few days later the cyst disappeared and it has never returned. That healing occurred over 30 years ago.

In my friend's self healing I believe that he gave a powerful emotional order to his subconscious mind, the area of the mind that controls all the body functions. The subconscious had no other choice but do as it was told.

WAVE A WAND

There are a large number of persons who are called dowsers, some 12,000 are members of the American Society of Dowsers. There are thousands more in the British Society of Dowsers. These people use a device such as a pendulum, L-rod, Y-rod or a wand - to name a few - to obtain information. To locate good drinking water a dowser will use his tool, usually a Y-rod, to find the location and to determine the depth and quantity of water desired. The skill is also used to locate a potential oil well or to find a lost person.

I was first introduced to the art of dowsing by an Episcopal minister in England who had not long before located a lost airplane in the jungle of South Africa. He used a process call map dowsing.

When you first watch a dowser work, particularly in the field looking for water, your skepticism is par with your curiosity. For example, a dowser after exploring a field will drive a stake in the ground and state, "Dig your well here, exactly at this spot. You will find a minimum of 5 gallons of good drinking water at 56 feet." When you put in your well where the stake was and find, as predict-ed, water at almost 56 feet with a delivery of over five gallons per minute, you need no further convincing.

In my own practice as a dowser, I primarily use the pendulum to obtain personality characteristics. I have diagnosed thousands of persons, identifying harmful psy-chological and spirit influences acting upon them. As there are no limits to the power of the mind, I can render harmless such influences. This is all done at a distance, not in the presence of the patient. This subject is covered in exacting detail in my book, *Exorcism.*

Our ever increasing technology in electronics and in the production of electrical energy, has made us vulnerable to injurious radiation. A dowser using an L- rod or a pendulum can detect harmful radiation, such as emanating from a color television set or from a high voltage transmission line. Such radiation can usually be verified by instrumentation. There are other harmful radiations originating underground such as from deep running streams of water or from deposits of uranium in the rocks below. Such radiation is said to be cancer producing and can be detected by a skilled dowser. Often the dowser can neutralize such harmful radiation.

As one explanation of the dowsing phenomena, it is conceivable that all information and knowledge is available in the Superconscious Mind. Please refer to Chapter 1. When a dowser asks a question of his dowsing device he is tapping into this Intelligence. The prearranged signal from his instrument indicates the answer.

I have found that most people who try one of the dowsing tools will get a dowsing response. Although one may learn the art on his own, it is usually better to use an instructor. There are dowsing chapters in each state where such instruction is available.

For further information write to the American Society of Dowsers, Inc., Danville, VT 05828-0024

TAKING A TRIP?

The power of our thoughts go far beyond our present life on this earth plane. There is substantial evidence that the laws we experience on this side differ little from the laws we may expect to find when we make our transition. Since there is no time on that other side, what we think is instantly produced. Let's not take a chance on being unprepared. We all have had enough trouble on this side due to our negative thinking. We have time now to learn to control our thoughts for positive results. Let's develop the habit of attracting what is beneficial to us on this plane. The habit may be very useful to us when we unpack our bags at our next destination.

TO BE CONTINUED

In summary, your Power of Thought is a continuous process, bringing forth positive or negative results. You are always controling that thought and directing what happens to you and, to a certain extent, what happens to others. Keeping a clear, positive mental picture of what you want with a strong belief that it is attainable, will unquestionably result in its materialization.

Our mind is a powerful tool when we control it.

We may wish to question the extent of this Power. Can we direct our mind to the great problems of today such as the problems of drug and alcohol, crime and disease and the poverty and homelessness of millions? Can our mind influence disasters and their effects on people, such as hurricanes, earthquakes, floods, mud slides, volcanic eruptions and devastating forest fires? Can our thoughts finally put to bed false ideas which have been perpetrated by rulers, nations, churches and organizations of wealth and power?

Using some of the ideas in this book, may I suggest that you can be instrumental in influencing in a positive way some of the problems expressed above.

Our medical establishment, contributed to and controlled by giant pharmaceutical companies, is firmly indoctrinated in using drugs to heal. In this country a medical doctor will lose his license if he deviates too far by substituting natural remedies for chemical ones. All too often, the doctor is looked upon as God, the final answer to one's physical or mental health. A false idea? Yes, but it will take a revolution in the health community before a positive change can take place.

Progress is being made in some areas. After over 40 years there is a movement in Europe to shed an idealogy that was unrealistic and unworkable. Finally, the East-bloc nations have freed themselves from Soviet armed intervention and are casting off the myth of communism forced upon them.

One last thought: Do you really want to prove to yourself that this stuff works? Try changing the weather. Perhaps you would like it to rain? Perhaps you would like the rain to stop when you reach your destination? It will be an interesting experiment.

BIBLIOGRAPHY

1. Anderson, U.S., *Three Magic Words,* 1974, Wilshire Book Co, 12015 Sherman Road, North Hollywood, CA 91605

2. Anderson, U.S., *The Secret of Secrets,* 1977, Wilshire Book Co., 12015 Sherman Road, North Hollywood, CA 91605

3. Barker, Raymond Charles, *Treat Yourself to Life,* 1954, Dodd, Mead & Company, 79 Madison Ave., New York, NY 10016

4. Barker, Raymond Charles, *You Are Invisible,* 1973, Dodd, Mead & Company, 79 Madison Ave., New York, NY 10016

5. Behrend, Genevieve, *Your Invisible Power,* 1951, DeVorss & Co., Publishers, P.O. Box 550, Marina Del Rey, CA 90294

6. Besant, Annie, *Thought Power,* 1973, The Theosophical Publishing House, P.O. Box 270, Wheaton, Il 60187

7. Bristol, Claude M., *The Magic of Believing,* 1948, Simon & Schuster, Inc., 630 Fifth Avenue, New York, NY 10029

8. Coomer, Bill, *Words to Live By,* 1994, Bill Coomer, 1024 South Benton, Cape Girardeau, MO 63701

9. Cox, Bill, *Techniques of Pendulum Dowsing,* 1977, Bill & Davina Cox, P.O. Box 30561, Santa Barbara, CA 93130

10. Edward, Harry, *A Guide to the Understanding and Practice of Spiritual Healing,* 1974, The Healer Publishing Company, Ltd., Burrows Lea, Guildford, Surrey, England.

11. Edward, Harry, *The Mediumship of Jack Webber,* 1962, The Healer Publishing Company, Burrows Lea, Guildford, Surrey, England.

12. Johnson, Tom, *Your Are Always Your Own Experience,* 1986, Los Arboles Publishing, P.O. Box 7000-54, Redondo Beach, CA 90277

13. Harris, Thomas A., M.D., *I'm OK-You're OK,* 1969, Avon Books, 959 Eight Avenue, New York, NY 10019

14. Holliwell, Raymond, Ph.D., *Working With the Law,* 1964, School of Christian Philosophy, 3121 N. 60th St., Phoenix, AZ

15. Holmes, Ernest, Ph.D., *Science of Mind,* 1938, 44th Printing, Dodd Mead and Co., 79 Madison Ave., New York, NY 10016

16. Ingraham, E.V., *Wells of Abundance,* 1966, DeVorss & Co., Publishers, P.O. Box 550, Marina Del Rey, CA 90294

17. Kramer, Edward L., *The Negative Power of Positive Thinking,* 1971, Successful Achievement, Inc., Lexington, KY 40502

18. Long, Max Freedom, *The Secret Science Behind Miracles,* 1948, DeVorss & Co., Publishers, P.O. Box 550, Marina Del Rey, CA 90294

19. Maltz, Maxwell, M.D., *Psycho-Cybernetics,* 1960, Simon & Schuster, Rockefeller Center, 630 Fifth Avenue, NY, NY 10020

20. Maurey, Eugene, *Exorcism,* 1989, Schiffer Publishing Ltd., 77 Lower Valley Road, Rt. 372, Atglen, PA 19310

21. Maurey, Eugene, *Forward Observer,* 1994, Midwest Books, 4555 W. 60th St. Chicago, Il 60629

22. Murphy, Joseph, Ph.D., *The Amazing Laws of Cosmic Mind Power,* 1973, Warner Books, Inc., 315 Park Ave. South, NY, NY 10010

23. Murphy, Joseph, Ph.D., *How to Attract Money,* 1955, DeVorss & Co., Publishers, P.O. Box 550, Marina Del Rey, CA 90294

24. Murphy, Joseph, Ph.D., *Within You Is the Power,* 1977, DeVorss & Co., Publishers, P.O. Box 550, Marina Del Rey, CA 90294

25. Norvell, Anthony, *The Million Dollar Secret that Lies Hidden within Your Mind,* 1963, Prentice-Hall, Inc., Englewood Cliffs, NJ 07632

26. Osborn, Alex, L.H.D., *Applied Imagination,* 1963, Charles Scribner's Sons, 866 3rd Avenue, New York, NY 10022

27. Pace, Eric, G., *Don't Just Sit There-Live!,* 1976, Harper & Row, Publishers, New York, NY 10022

28. Peale, Norman Vincent, *You Can if You Think You Can,* 1974, Fawcett Publications, P.O. Box 1014, Greenwich, CT 06830

29. Pilgrim, Peace, *An Autobiography,* 1983, Compiled by her friends, Ocean Tree Press, P.O. Box 1295, Santa Fe, NM 10020

30. Schwartz, David Joseph, Ph.D., *The Magic of Thinking Big,* 1982, Simon & Schuster Publishers, 1230 Avenue of the Americas, New York, NY 10020

31. Sherman, Harold, *How to Foresee and Control Your Future,* 1970, Fawcett Publications, P.O. Box 1014, Greenwich, CT 06830

32. Sherman, Harold, *Know Your Own Mind,* 1971, Fawcett Publications, P.O. Box 1014, Greenwich, CT 06830

33. Sherman, Harold, *The New TNT Miraculous Power Within You,* 1966, Prentice-Hall, Inc., Englewood Cliffs, NJ 07632

34. Sherman, Harold, *Wonder Healers of the Philippines,* 1967, Psychic Press Ltd. 23 Great Queen Street, London, W.C.2, England

35. Speller, Jon, Ph.D., *Seed Money In Action,* 1986, Morning Star Press, P.O. Box 1095, Grand Central Station, NY, NY 10163

36. Stone, W. Clement, & Hill, Napoleon, *Success Through a Positive Mental Attitude,* 1987, Simon & Schuster, Inc., 1230 Avenue of the Americas, New York, NY 10020

37. Taylor, Richard, *Metaphysics,* 1963, Prentice Hall, Inc. Englewood Cliffs, NJ

38. Thomas, Arthur G., *Abundance Is Your Right,* 1977, DeVorss & Co., Publishers, P.O. Box 550, Marina del Rey, CA 90294

39. Troward, Thomas, *The Hidden Power,* 1921, Dodd, Mead and Co., 79 Madison Avenue, New York, NY 10016

40. Troward, Thomas, *The Law and the Word,* 1917, Dodd, Mead and Co., 79 Madison Avenue, New York, NY 10016

41. Tyler, Paula J., *New Age Metaphysics,* 1987, Metaphysical Enterprises, Box 168, Eureka Springs, AR 72632

EXORCISM

by Eugene Maurey

This book explains how a depossession is performed at a distance, not in the presence of the client. It traces the normal progression that a dying person experiences. It explains the reasons why often a normal death does not occur, resulting in the spirit of the dead person becoming earthbound. It then relates how some spirits, desiring to continue an earth-life antisocial existence, will seek out and possess a living person, resulting in a great deal of trouble to that person and often death.

The exorcist must have an understanding of the environment and the situation in which the earthbound spirit finds himself. The laws governing the spirit world are clearly defined in this book and become useful tools during an exorcism. The pendulum is used to obtain reliable information about the intruding spirits.

When the principles of an exorcism are understood, the procedure is comparably simple. The author fully explains the method of performing an exorcism at a distance. It is safe and effective.

Some 40 case histories are described. Most are from the author's personal experience and some from the practice of contemporaries or historical accounts.

The results of a remote exorcism can be said to be miraculous. The alcoholic abruptly ceases his heavy drinking and begins to lead a normal life. The drug abuser has no further interest in drugs. The criminal no longer continues his unlawful activities. A person diagnosed with a serious physical disease, frequently finds himself free of it almost overnight.

When a person carefully follows the principles and suggestions given in this book, he/she can effectively detoxify dozens or perhaps hundreds of people of alcohol or drug addiction.

MIDWEST BOOKS 4555 W. 60th St. CHICAGO, IL. 60629 $12.95

FORWARD OBSERVER
by Eugene Maurey, Captain, Field Artillery

As a artillery liaison officer with the infantry and forward observer during World War II, from the beaches of Normandy to the liberation of Czechoslovakia, Eugene Maurey served with front line troops in the 79th Infantry Division. This division often found itself the spearhead of the drive through France, Belgium and Germany. The division took 150 percent casualties. During the breakout in Normandy 180 men infantry companies found themselves down to 20 and 40 men.

This is a personal account of the individual actions more often never recorded nor even noted as most of the participants became casualties. The book speaks about the GI in his foxhole, his fears and courage during an attack and his constant weariness, but also his moment of play when the pressure let up.

What is unusual about this book is the unexpected coincidences which kept occurring to the author. There were numerous near misses from artillery shells and small arms fire. In some instances it appeared that he led a charmed life by extracting himself and those with him from seemingly impossible highly dangerous situations.

This is not a history book nor is it a biography. It simply is a vivid picture how it was with the GI on the front line. It is highly possible that it differs little from the foot soldier of wars which have been fought before and since World War II.

MIDWEST BOOKS $12.95
4555 W. 60TH STREET, CHICAGO, IL 60629